D1481835

THE ONCE IN A
Blue Moon
Boot Bus

Rebecca Ondov Blasing

Illustrated by Lynda Cohen

To my best friend, Jesus Christ
R.B.

To Chuck and Jordan
L.C.

Faith Kids® is an imprint of Cook Communications Ministries,
Colorado Springs, Colorado 80918
Cook Communications, Paris, Ontario
Kingsway Communications, Eastbourne, England

THE ONCE IN A BLUE MOON BOOT BUS
©2000 by Rebecca Ondov Blasing for text and Lynda Cohen for illustrations

Edited by Kathy Davis
Designed by Ron Kadrmas

First printing, 2000
Printed in Singapore
04 03 02 01 00   5 4 3 2 1

Library of Congress Cataloging-in-Publication Data

"Good night, Mom," Bobby said as he pulled Grandma's quilt under his chin.

He giggled as his mom kissed the tip of his nose. "Do you really think the Once in a Blue Moon Boot Bus will have boots for me?"

"Mr. Hush will be driving tomorrow. Maybe he'll help you find something," said Bobby's mom as she quietly closed the door.

Bobby clutched his wallet to his chest. In it was every cent he'd earned raking leaves and feeding the calves; now there was enough money to buy his first pair of *real* boots. Tomorrow he wouldn't have to wear his dirty old tennies any more—the Once in a Blue Moon Boot Bus was coming!

Bobby's heart thumped as he thought about the rickety old blue bus that crawled through the prairies of Montana and wound through the mountains of Wyoming, selling boots to the ranchers who lived miles away from any town. Inside the bus, shelves brimmed with every kind of boot imaginable—and in every size.

**The full moon cast mountain-like shadows on the wall.
Visions of different kinds of boots appeared in Bobby's mind.**
Hmmm . . . maybe hiking boots, **he thought.**

"Boys and girls, I'm Gush Struck, host of 'Kids'
Greatest Adventures.' I'm hovering over Pikes Peak.
We're watching to see if Bobby Muse will set a world
record for being the youngest person to climb all of
Colorado's Fourteeners. Come on Bobby . . . just a
couple of steps more! He did it! Bobby Muse holds the
world record!"

**As the moonlight rippled across the bedroom floor, it
highlighted a pair of grubby shoes. Bobby winced. "I** *could* **be
a famous mountain climber . . . if I didn't have to wear those
dumb tennies."**

The next morning Bobby woke up early and ran to the window. Nope, no bus yet. Stuffing his wallet into his back pocket, he slid down the stair railing.

Bouncing into the kitchen he asked, "Mom, where's the Once in a Blue Moon Boot Bus?"

"Bobby, the sun just came up!" His mom wiped her hands on her apron. "Eat your breakfast, then help your dad with the chores. The bus will be here before you know it."

The TV blared as Bobby spooned down his cereal.

"Boys and girls, I'm Gush Struck and today I'm hosting 'Kids' Greatest Adventures' featuring lion tamers under the age of ten."

For the next half-hour Bobby glued himself to the program, imagining that he stood in the circus ring with the enormous cats. When his mom clicked off the TV, Bobby slipped on his dirty shoes and mumbled, "I *could* be a famous lion tamer . . . if I didn't have to wear these dumb tennies."

As his dad drove across the bumpy pasture, Bobby tossed out hay. He watched two calves spin around, bucking and kicking. *Hmmm . . . cowboy boots.*

"Gush Struck here. Today I'm sitting ringside to the largest rodeo of the year—the World Champion Bull-Riding Competition.

"Wow! Look at that bull buck and spin. Bobby's getting jerked all over, but he's hanging on—there's the buzzer! The new World Champion Bull Rider is Bobby Muse!"

The pickup hit a bump, jolting Bobby back to reality. "I *could* be a famous bull rider . . . if I didn't have to wear these dumb tennies."

Bobby carried oats to the horses' feed bunk. Old Shoe, the Belgian draft horse, tried to dip his nose in the bucket. Bobby pulled it away, lost his balance, and stepped into a mud puddle.

"Old Shoe, get out of the way!" yelled Bobby. A tear rolled down his cheek as he looked down at his muddy shoes. His big toe stuck out.

He stomped his foot and said, "How can I be famous when I have to wear these things?"

A smile slithered across Bobby's face. Soon the Once in a Blue Moon Boot Bus would be there! Bobby imagined walking over to the trash and throwing away his old tennies.

Walking back to the house, Bobby saw a man fishing in the creek. *Hmmm . . . hip boots,* **he thought.**

"Boys and girls, this is Gush Struck. I'm standing beside a blue-ribbon trout stream. That's Bobby Muse in the river, whipping his fly-fishing line through the air. Whew! Did you see that? The trout grabbed the fly in midair. Look at him play that fish. It's huge . . . let's measure. Bobby Muse holds the new world record!"

The applause of the cameramen was so loud that it rumbled the ground. *Could that be . . . thunder? Nope—no clouds in the sky.* **Bobby stood still. A cloud of dust drew a line in the air above the dirt road. Then a faded patch of blue peeked through the cloud.**

Bobby ran down the lane waving his arms. "Stop, Mr. Hush. Stop!"

The Once in a Blue Moon Boot Bus snorted to a stop. Mr. Hush squeaked the doors open. A grin parted his straggly beard as he nodded for Bobby to climb aboard.

Mr. Hush perched a pair of half-moon reading glasses on the tip of his nose and settled back to read his newspaper.

Bobby charged up the steps.

It was true! Rows of boots—all sizes and colors—stood on shelves higher than Bobby's head. Bobby had never seen so many boots.

He walked down the row, tapping his fingers across the toes of the boots: logging boots, cowboy boots, and ski boots; hiking boots, army boots, and wading boots; telephone-pole climber's boots, and dancing boots—yuck, who'd want to dance with girls?

Bobby ripped off his tennies and started pulling on boots. Too short . . . too long . . . too tight . . . too loose.

Bobby squealed when he discovered a pair of fireman's boots. Quickly he pulled them on.

"Gush Struck here, standing before a real inferno. This house is consumed by flames, and a little girl is trapped inside. Listen . . . the siren.

"Look, it's Bobby Muse hanging off the back of the truck. He's jumping off . . . and running through the flames! He's got the girl . . . and they're safe! Our hero, Bobby Muse!"

"Look at me! I'm a famous fireman," said Bobby.
Mr. Hush lowered his newspaper and looked over the top
of his glasses. "Hrumph," he said.

Bobby threw the fireman's boots aside and climbed up to the next shelf. Too short . . . too long . . . too tight . . . too loose.

None of the boots fit, and he'd already tried on all the boots on one whole side of the bus! *I've got to find something!* thought Bobby.

As the morning sun rose higher, the bus got hotter and hotter, and stuffier and stuffier.

Down the other side went Bobby. Too short . . . too long . . . too tight . . . too loose.

"Wow, look at these," shouted Bobby as he yanked on a pair of snowboard boots.

"Gush Struck here. This is the final run of the Olympic snowboard competition. Whoa, there's Bobby Muse. Look how effortlessly he carves down that cliff face. Here come the others . . . they're neck and neck . . . Bobby takes the lead. Bobby Muse is the new Olympic gold medalist!"

"Look at me! I'm a famous Olympic snowboarder," said Bobby.

Mr. Hush lowered his newspaper and looked over the top of his glasses. "Hrumph," was all he said.

A horrible thought struck Bobby: *What if I don't find any boots, and I have to wear these tennies forever?*

He scrambled over the mountain of boots and frantically jerked on more boots. Too short . . . too long . . . too tight . . . too loose.

Tears rolled down Bobby's cheeks as he pulled on the last pair of boots. "This can't be. I've tried on logging boots, cowboy boots, and ski boots; hiking boots, army boots, and wading boots; telephone-pole climber's boots, and *even* dancing boots, and nothing fits!"

Bobby tore off the boots and flung them into the corner. They landed on something in a heap. Another pair of boots? Bobby scuttled over. *Sandals?*

Carrying the sandals like a dead mouse, he marched up to Mr. Hush. "These don't belong here! This is a boot bus!"

"Hrumph," said Mr. Hush as he lowered his newspaper and peered over the top of his glasses. "The greatest man who ever lived wore a pair of sandals. He never won a gold medal or appeared on TV. He never won a rodeo or was a celebrity."

Mr. Hush folded his newspaper and tucked his glasses into his shirt pocket. "Well, Bobby, more folks have followed the footprints made by His sandals than any boots ever sewn—and the wonderful thing is they still do."

"He wasn't famous?" asked Bobby.

"No," replied Mr. Hush. "But He was great."

"Could I be great . . . and not be famous?"

"Yup," said Mr. Hush. "This man healed the sick and helped the poor. He fed 5,000 folks with only five loaves of bread and two fish. He did miracles— flat out miracles."

Bobby had never seen Mr. Hush excited about anything before, nor heard him talk so much.

Mr. Hush stroked his beard. "But the biggest miracle He did, He did for you and me. He loved us so much that He let His enemies nail Him to the cross as a sacrifice to pay for our sins."

"Jesus? Jesus wore sandals like these?" asked Bobby.

"Yup," said Mr. Hush. "But it takes more than just sandals to make you great, it takes living like He did. As they say, 'walking the walk.'"

Bobby plopped down on the floor and buckled on the sandals—a perfect fit. Perhaps they were made just for him.

As Bobby skipped down the steps he yelled, "Look at me! Who needs fancy boots to leave footprints that last forever!"

Tidbits About Blue Moons

Do you wonder why the bus was called the Once in a Blue Moon Boot Bus or why people say "once in a blue moon"?

The most recent meaning of blue moon came into usage in 1946. A blue moon is the second full moon in a single calendar month. It happens so rarely that in 100 years only 41 months (out of 1,200) will have two full moons. If you average it out, there will be a blue moon every two-and-a-half years.

The other meaning is: When a season contains four full moons, instead of three, the third moon is called a blue moon.

Either way, blue moons are so rare, people started using the expression "once in a blue moon" to mean "it's not going to happen too soon." That's how the bus got its name— it rarely rumbled past Bobby's ranch.

Does the moon really turn blue? Find the answer to this—as well as when to look for the next blue moon—on the Web site: www.obliquity.com/astro/bluemoon.html.

The Once in a Blue Moon Boot Bus

Ages: 4-7

Life Issue: I want my child to learn to make wise decisions.

Spiritual Building Block: Wisdom

Sight: Help your child make a footprints poster for his or her room. Using a large piece of poster board, have your child stand barefoot while you trace around his or her feet. Trace three or four "footsteps" that your child can then color in. Label each step with a characteristic of Jesus: loving others, trusting God, helping people, praying daily, or others that you think of together. Title the poster: I Can Walk in Jesus' Steps. Place the poster where your child can see it every day.

Sound: Help your child learn to ask the question: What would Jesus do? Explain that we need to ask that question about our choices if we want to walk in Jesus' steps. Practice asking the question using the following imaginary situations:

• Your friend is playing at your house with your toys. He or she accidentally breaks a toy. What do you do?

• You are ready for bed, but your room seems extra dark and full of scary shadows. You feel afraid. What do you do?

• Your mom is very busy trying to put the groceries away. You can see that she is tired and in a hurry. What do you do?

Touch: Play a game of "Whose Shoes?" Gather shoes from various family members, in a variety of sizes, and pile them on the floor. Blindfold your child with a scarf. Have your child try on shoes without looking and see if he or she can guess whom the shoes belong to. Be sure to hand your child his own shoe for the final guess. Say, "Why does that last shoe feel just right? Because it is yours! Bigger shoes don't fit because your feet haven't grown enough yet." Explain that we want to grow to be like Jesus and learn to walk in His shoes. That takes time. But trying to follow Jesus each day will help us grow in our hearts, and we will be more like Him every day.